THE HEART THAT GREW THREE SIZES
YOUTH STUDY BOOK

The Heart That Grew Three Sizes:
Finding Faith in the Story of the Grinch

The Heart That Grew Three Sizes
978-1-7910-1732-3
978-1-7910-1733-0 eBook

The Heart That Grew Three Sizes: Leader Guide
978-1-7910-1734-7
978-1-7910-1735-4 eBook

The Heart That Grew Three Sizes: DVD
978-1-7910-1736-1

The Heart That Grew Three Sizes: Youth Study Book
978-1-7910-1741-5
978-1-7910-1742-2 eBook

The Heart That Grew Three Sizes: Children's Leader Guide
978-1-7910-1745-3

The Heart That Grew Three Sizes: Worship Resources
978-1-7910-1743-9 Flash Drive
978-1-7910-1744-6 Download

Also by Matt Rawle

The Faith of a Mockingbird
The Salvation of Doctor Who
Hollywood Jesus
The Redemption of Scrooge
What Makes a Hero?
The Gift of the Nutcracker
The Grace of Les Miserables

With Magrey R. deVega, Ingrid McIntyre, and April Casperson
Almost Christmas

For more information, visit MattRawle.com.

MATT RAWLE

THE HEART THAT GREW THREE SIZES

YOUTH
STUDY BOOK
by Josh Tinley

FINDING FAITH IN
THE STORY OF THE GRINCH

ABINGDON PRESS | NASHVILLE

The Heart That Grew Three Sizes:
Finding Faith in the Story of the Grinch
Youth Study Book

978-1-7910-1741-5

21 22 23 24 25 26 27 28 29 30 — 10 9 8 7 6 5 4 3 2 1
MANUFACTURED IN THE UNITED STATES OF AMERICA

CONTENTS

CONTENTS

INTRODUCTION

"You're a mean one, Mr. Grinch."

Those six words are the opening line, and title, of a song that is nearly impossible to avoid during November or December of any given year. The song—composed for a 1966 animated holiday television special—describes a creature who is nasty and vile with termites in his smile and garlic in his soul.

This creature, the Grinch, lives outside the town of Whoville and is infamous for his attempt to steal the town's Christmas celebration. The Grinch, at least as we know him today, first appeared in the 1957 book *How the Grinch Stole Christmas!* by Dr. Seuss. Since then, the book has been published in several languages, there have been multiple television and movie adaptations of the story, and the Grinch himself is featured on Christmas tree ornaments and lawn decorations. *Grinch* has joined *Scrooge* as a nickname for anyone who gets grumpy during the holiday season or doesn't get excited about the pageantry surrounding Christmas.

Dr. Seuss wrote *How the Grinch Stole Christmas!* to express his concerns about the commercialization of Christmas. The book teaches us that Christmas isn't really about gifts and decorations, but about relationships. In the end, the villainous Grinch has a change of heart and celebrates Christmas with the people of Whoville.

Even though *How the Grinch Stole Christmas!* has been a part of our culture for more than sixty years, our culture has not fully embraced its message. For many, Christmas is an opportunity to turn a profit or to get new stuff. For others, the Christmas season comes with a lengthy to-do list and pressure to make everything just right.

For followers of Christ the weeks leading up to Christmas belong to the Advent season, a time of preparation when we look forward—and backward—to all the ways that Christ enters our world. We prepare to celebrate Jesus's birth in Bethlehem; we anticipate Christ's promised return; and we open our eyes, ears, and hearts to all the ways that Jesus is present with us now. During these weeks of preparation, we can learn much from the Grinch's story about staying focused on our relationships with God and with others amid the distractions of the holiday season.

This youth study book is meant to accompany *The Heart That Grew Three Sizes*, by Matt Rawle. Through his engaging and insightful reflections, Rawle highlights a number of faith themes in Dr. Seuss's book *How the Grinch Stole Christmas!* Rawle helps us understand that our culture can point us to God, because Christ came to redeem all of human life and experience, which includes things like art, writing, and music. When we pay attention to them, even secular stories and expressions have something to teach us about God and the hope that Christ brings. Through his writing, Rawle primes our imaginations to see the connections between the Grinch's story and our faith, the many touchpoints connecting Scripture with Dr. Seuss's story, and how the Grinch's transformation points to the transformation God promises us in Jesus Christ.

The Grinch's story points to the reality that what we celebrate at Christmas—the peace, hope, love, and joy that Christ promises—is something more than gifts, food, and decorations. These things are intangible, transformative, and eternal. It also highlights the possibility of redemption and transformation, as the Whos' celebration of Christmas ultimately causes the Grinch's heart to grow three sizes, as well as the power of forgiveness as the Whos receive the Grinch and seat him at the head of the table when he returns what he stole from them.

While this youth study book contains everything needed for a four-week study based on Matt's insights, youth are encouraged to read the main book as well. *The Heart That Grew Three Sizes*, by Matt Rawle, contains a number of valuable lessons and insights that will enrich your experience of the Advent season and help your faith in Christ to grow and mature.

This study includes four sessions:

Session 1: When Everything Is Wrong

Despite its reputation as a time of joy, the Christmas season (and the Advent season leading up to it) is for many a time of turmoil. How do we work through the stress, envy, and disappointment that so often accompany our celebrations? And what can we learn from the story of the Grinch and the people of Whoville?

9

Session 2: When Christmas Isn't Christmas

The Grinch didn't really steal Christmas. He took lights, decorations, and presents. He even took food. But he didn't take away Christmas. Christmas, he discovered, is in the hearts and relationships of those who celebrate it. Too often we get so caught up in the pageantry of Christmas that we forget about Christ, the one whose birth we're actually commemorating. What can the Grinch teach us about keeping our priorities straight during the Advent and Christmas seasons?

Session 3: When Light Shines

When the Grinch attempts to steal Christmas, he dresses as Santa Claus. Our traditions about Santa Claus involve accountability. He rewards well-behaved children and punishes naughty ones. As Christians, we serve a God who holds us accountable. But God doesn't punish our misbehavior by withholding gifts. God, through Christ and the Holy Spirit and our fellow Christians, works to redeem and transform us. How do we experience the same redemption and transformation that the Grinch does at the end of Dr. Seuss's book?

Session 4: When Joy Is Our Song

The Grinch tried to steal Christmas from Whoville, but on Christmas morning the Whos were still celebrating. Joy prevailed. Often the joy of Christmas gets lost among the stress, busyness, and frustration. How can we experience the same Christmas joy that we see on the final pages of *How the Grinch Stole Christmas!*?

USING THIS RESOURCE

This study can be used in Sunday school, during evening youth fellowship gatherings, or as part of a small group or midweek Bible study. There is not a separate leader guide for this study. All instructions for leaders and participants are found in this book. The leader of the study could be an adult or one of the student participants.

The four sessions of this study may correspond to the four Sundays of Advent, and of course the story *How the Grinch Stole Christmas!* is most popular in the weeks leading up to Christmas. But the themes that you will explore are not limited to the Advent and Christmas seasons. This study would be appropriate at any time of year, including just after Christmas break or during the summer as part of a "Christmas in Summer" event.

All four session plans include:

- A brief introduction, summarizing the key themes and learning goals of the session.
- A list of supplies that you will need for each session.
- Opening and closing discussion questions and prayers.
- A variety of discussion questions and learning activities.

The activities in each session, including the opening and closing, should take between 50 and 60 minutes. Every session has enough activities to extend the session beyond that time frame if you have interest or plan to meet longer.

Many activities instruct groups to break up into smaller teams. If you have five or fewer participants, do these activities as a single team.

A NOTE ON VIRTUAL MEETINGS

With some creativity and patience on everyone's part, you can adapt these sessions for virtual, online group study using such platforms as Zoom. Should you want or need to meet virtually:

- Communicate all online meeting details (websites, passwords, beginning time, and so on) to participants well in advance of each session. Create and use an email distribution list, putting your study's name in the subject line so recipients can spot and refer to the email easily. If possible, post contact information for your study (but not each session's log-in information) on your congregation's website.

- If using video in your virtual meeting, be sure you, as leader, are sitting in a well-lit and quiet place in front of a background with few or no distractions. Encourage group participants to do likewise.

- Agree with your members on a group protocol for recognizing who "has the floor." For example, will participants agree to wait until no one is speaking to answer a question? Will they need to "raise their hand" (physically or digitally) before speaking? Establishing and sticking with some basic ground rules will make your virtual discussions go more smoothly and be more enjoyable and productive.

Most of the activities listed in this study can be easily adapted for virtual meetings. For those involving recording responses on a marker-board or large sheet of paper, you can use Zoom's "screen share" feature (or equivalent on a different platform) to display a document where you write down group members' answers. For writing or drawing activities that require supplies, each participant will need to provide their own paper, pens or pencils, and other materials. Be sure to send instructions about the supplies needed ahead of time, so that participants can have them ready before your meeting.

Session 1

WHEN EVERYTHING IS WRONG

In the 1950s Theodor Geisel, better known as Dr. Seuss, set out to write a Christmas story that wasn't as sentimental or corny as most of our culture's beloved Christmas tales. He came up with the Grinch, a grumpy character who, like Seuss, didn't care for a lot of the decorations, music, and traditions that accompany Christmas.

The result, *How the Grinch Stole Christmas!*, was one of Seuss's best known and most beloved books. It has been translated into several languages and adapted into two major motion pictures, a Broadway musical, and a very popular 1966 television special. On its surface the Grinch is a critique of the commercialization of Christmas. But when we look beneath the surface, we find that it has many other lessons to teach us.

GETTING READY

For this session you will need:

- Bibles
- A markerboard or large sheet of paper
- Markers
- Pens or pencils

POP QUIZ (5-10 MINUTES)

As participants arrive, discuss your level of familiarity with Dr. Seuss's *How the Grinch Stole Christmas!* Did you read the book as a child or have you read it to children? Have you watched the animated television special featuring Boris Karloff as both the Grinch and the narrator? Is "You're a Mean One, Mr. Grinch" on your Christmas music playlist? Have you seen the live-action film directed by Ron Howard? Is watching one of the Grinch movies an annual holiday tradition?

When most are present and have had a chance to join in the discussion, see who knows the answers to the following Grinch-related questions.

1. What is the birth name of Dr. Seuss, author of *How the Grinch Stole Christmas!*?
2. When was *How the Grinch Stole Christmas!* published?
3. According to Dr. Seuss, what real person was the inspiration for the Grinch character?

4. In what year did the *How the Grinch Stole Christmas!* animated television special first air?
5. Who portrayed the Grinch in the 2000 theatrical film, *How the Grinch Stole Christmas!*?
6. What was the name of the 2017 animated film based on *How the Grinch Stole Christmas!*?
7. Who was the voice of the Grinch in the 2017 movie?

Answers are on page 61.

IT'S THE MOST WONDERFUL TIME OF THE YEAR? *(10 MINUTES)*

Supplies: Bibles, paper, pens or pencils

Invite a participant to read aloud:

> Many popular Christmas songs describe the holiday season as a "wonderful" or "jolly" time, and families, churches, and businesses often go out of their way to create a joyful and festive atmosphere with lights and other decorations. But there are plenty of people for whom the Advent and Christmas seasons are not the "most wonderful time of the year."

Divide into teams of three or four. Each team should create two lists. The first list should include things that are wonderful about the Advent and Christmas seasons—things that one would look forward to. The second list should include things related to this time of year that aren't so wonderful—things that might cause pain or stress or annoyance.

Teams should spend about five minutes on these lists. Then invite a representative from each team to read aloud his or her team's lists for the group.

17

Discuss:

- What, if anything, surprised you about these lists?
- Which things, if any, appeared on both lists?

Ask a participant to read aloud:

> By the first Sunday of Advent, most churches have decorated their sanctuaries, festive holiday music can be heard on store intercoms and car stereos, and people are busy buying Christmas presents or making wish lists. Amid all of this joy and celebration, we read Scriptures such as Isaiah 64:1-9.
>
> Isaiah 64 was written during what is known as the postexilic period. Decades earlier the Babylonians had conquered Jerusalem and taken many of God's people into exile. At the time of Isaiah 64, God's people had returned to the Promised Land to rebuild their nation. But returning home posed new and unexpected challenges. God's people soon found themselves crying out for the God who had done so much for them in the past.

Invite one or two volunteers to read aloud Isaiah 64:1-4, 7-9.

Discuss:

- What do these verses say about the author's understanding of God?
- What do these verses tell us about God's people?

Ask a participant to read aloud:

> In *How the Grinch Stole Christmas!*, Dr. Seuss describes the Grinch's heart as being "two sizes too small." He's sad and

frustrated, and we don't know exactly why. God's people in Isaiah 64 find themselves in a similar situation. Even though they know what God has done for them and what God is capable of, they doubt themselves and worry that they have disappointed God. Most of us have also experienced this feeling. When we feel frustration and despair, we need reminders of God's presence and of what God is capable of.

Each person should write on a sheet of paper one example of how he or she has experienced God's power or presence. This could involve experiencing God through the natural world; feeling God's peace during a stressful time; getting an opportunity to use their God-given gifts or to show God's love to others; feeling the movement of the Holy Spirit during worship; or something else entirely.

Discuss:

- What do these examples teach us about what God is capable of?
- How can your experiences, and those of others, give you peace and hope during difficult times?

GREEN LIKE THE GRINCH?
(OPTIONAL, 10 MINUTES)

Ask participants each to do the following on a separate sheet of paper:

1. Write the name of the cereal Froot Loops. (Be sure not to reveal the actual spelling. The purpose is to see how many are aware that Kellogg's intentionally spells *fruit* incorrectly.)
2. Describe the color "chartreuse."

THE HEART THAT GREW THREE SIZES: YOUTH STUDY BOOK

3. Which of the following is the name of a popular brand of peanut butter, "Jiffy," "Jif," or "Jeff"?
4. What color is the Grinch in Dr. Seuss's *How the Grinch Stole Christmas!*?

Go through each of the four instructions, one at a time, inviting volunteers to show or read what they wrote. Then reveal the following:

1. The word *fruit* in the name of the cereal *Froot Loops* is intentionally misspelled as *Froot*.
2. Chartreuse is a yellow-green color similar to lime green. There's a common misconception that chartreuse is a pinkish-red color similar to magenta.
3. The name of the peanut butter is "Jif." But many people (and particularly users of the discussion-based website Reddit) have a memory of the brand name being "Jiffy," even though "Jiffy" has never been the name of a major peanut butter brand.
4. Black and white, with red eyes. In the original book, the Grinch's fur had no color.

Discuss whether anyone in the group is familiar with the "Mandela Effect." The Mandela Effect describes when a large number of people remember something that did not happen or remember something differently than it actually occurred. The effect is named for South African anti-Apartheid leader, and eventual president, Nelson Mandela. Many people have a vivid memory of Mandela dying in prison in the 1980s when, in reality, he was released from prison in 1990, became president in 1994, and died in 2013 at the age of 95.

The color of the Grinch's fur in Dr. Seuss's book is an example of the Mandela Effect. Because the Grinch had green (or chartreuse) fur in the 1966 television special, and in later adaptations and Grinch-related

WHEN EVERYTHING IS WRONG

merchandise, many people have a false memory of him being green in the original book.

Invite a participant to read aloud:

> Even though the Grinch was originally black-and-white, not green, his fur color in movies and television specials is appropriate because the color green traditionally represents envy.

GREEN WITH ENVY (5-10 MINUTES)

Supplies: Bibles

Discuss:

- Are you familiar with the phrase "green with envy"? If so, what, do you think, does it mean for someone to be green with envy?
- For that matter, what is envy?
- How can envy be dangerous or destructive?
- Describe a time when you were envious of someone, even if you tried not to be.

Explain that, while envy is a common human response, it can lead to resentment and rage and broken relationships if it is not dealt with.

Invite one or two volunteers to read aloud Matthew 2:1-12.

Discuss:

- What do the magi, or wise men, ask about when they visit King Herod?
- What is Herod's emotional reaction to the magi's question?

21

- What does Herod actually know about the "newborn king of the Jews" the magi are referring to?
- Why, do you think, does Herod seem so envious of a king he knows nothing about?
- What instructions does God give the magi regarding King Herod?

King Herod in these verses is Herod the Great, who ruled the territory that had once been the kingdoms of Israel and Judah from about 37 BCE until about 4 BCE. Herod considered himself the king of the Jews, but he was a puppet king who was ruling on Rome's behalf. He got the job because his father had connections with Julius Caesar. Herod ruled as a brutal dictator; most of the Jewish people neither liked nor supported him.

Volunteers should read aloud Matthew 2:13-18, which describes how Herod acted on his envy.

Discuss:

- When has envy caused you to do or say something that was hurtful or that you would later regret? (Don't pressure participants to share anything they are uncomfortable sharing.)
- How can you deal with envy so that it doesn't become hurtful?

A WONDERFUL, AWFUL IDEA
(10 MINUTES)

Supplies: Bibles, a markerboard or large sheet of paper, markers

As a group, brainstorm a list of archrivals and list them on a markerboard or large sheet of paper. This list could include sports rivals (individual or team), political rivals, or business rivals but should be limited to real-world examples. (Do not include fictional rivalries like Batman versus the Joker.)

After a few minutes of brainstorming, discuss:

- Which rivalries are you most invested in? (Do you support a pro or college sports team that has a heated rivalry with another team? Are you loyal to a brand that competes for customers with another brand?)
- When, if ever, has your investment in a rivalry caused you to be happy about someone else's misfortune? (For example, have you ever found yourself rooting for a team to lose or feeling satisfaction when someone fails or falls short of expectations?)

Invite a participant to read aloud:

In *How the Grinch Stole Christmas!*, the Grinch has "a wonderful, awful idea" of how to steal Christmas by dressing up as Santa Claus, disguising his dog as a reindeer, and stealing all Christmas presents and decorations from the town of Whoville. The Grinch hates Christmas so much that he takes satisfaction in spoiling other people's holiday celebrations.

In the spirit of not delighting in other people's failures and sufferings, come up with a way to compliment one of your rivals. (For example, "I respect that [sports team] has been able to maintain a winning culture for several decades," or, "Even though I disagree with [elected representative] on many issues, I know that she genuinely cares about our community.") Write this compliment at the top of the following page.

UNMET EXPECTATIONS (10-15 MINUTES)

Supplies: Bibles, pens or pencils, a markerboard or large sheet of paper, markers

Take a couple of minutes to reflect on a time when you were disappointed by something you'd been looking forward to. This could be an athletic contest or performance that you'd spent weeks preparing for and where everything seemed to go wrong. It could be a family vacation or a week at camp that was ruined by bad weather. With this in mind, fill in the two columns below.

What I Expected	What Actually Happened

After a few minutes, volunteers may present what they wrote. Then discuss:

- What did the Grinch expect to happen when he stole the Christmas presents and decorations from Whoville?
- The people of Whoville surprised the Grinch by rejoicing in spite of all that happened. When have you celebrated a situation that seemed bad on the surface?

Invite one or two volunteers to read aloud Luke 1:26-38.

As a group, list on a markerboard or large sheet of paper reasons why Mary should be afraid or upset about the news she has heard.

Next, invite one or two volunteers to read aloud Luke 1:39-49. (Elizabeth is described as a relative of Mary's. The baby in Elizabeth's belly is John the Baptist, the great prophet. Months earlier an angel had told Elizabeth that she would give birth to a son named John, despite being past her child-bearing years.)

Discuss:

- How do Mary and Elizabeth respond to the news that Mary will be having a baby?
- Why do they respond this way despite all of the difficulties and challenges that Mary will be facing?

Ask a participant to read aloud:

> In *How the Grinch Stole Christmas!* the residents of Whoville wake up on Christmas morning to find no gifts and no decorations, but they choose to celebrate anyway, because it is Christmas. Likewise, Mary knows that she will be facing tremendous challenges in the coming months and years. But she chooses to look forward with hope.

WHEN THERE IS NO PEACE
(10-15 MINUTES)

Supplies: Bibles, paper, pens or pencils

Invite a participant to read aloud:

> When he is "stealing Christmas," the Grinch takes all the Christmas lights that had been used as decorations. And, on his way out of Cindy Lou Who's house, the last thing the Grinch takes is the log from the fireplace. A big part of stealing Christmas is stealing light.

Divide participants into teams of three or four. Give teams exactly three minutes to list on a sheet of paper all the ways that lights are used in Advent and Christmas celebrations.

After three minutes, invite one team to read aloud its list. For each item on the list, a representative for any other team that has listed that item should raise a hand. All teams that have listed that answer should place an "x" by it. Then have a second team read aloud any items on its list without an "x." Continue until all teams have gone or until there are no more teams with original answers. See which team has come up with the most original answers.

Then ask:

- Why is light such an important part of Advent and Christmas celebrations?

Ask a volunteer to read aloud:

> The Grinch's efforts to take the light out of Christmas are unsuccessful. When the sun rises the next morning, he

> discovers the true light of Christmas is still shining. Even though their decorative and symbolic lights, from the strands of bulbs and the candles and the fireplaces, are gone, a greater light continues to shine in their hearts and their relationships.

Invite a volunteer to read aloud John 8:12.

Discuss:

- What do you think Jesus means when he refers to himself as "the light of the world"?
- In what ways does Jesus's light shine through the lives and relationships of his followers?

CLOSING (5-10 MINUTES)

Discuss:

- What is one thing you learned during our time together that you didn't know before?
- What is one thing that you will do in the coming week as a result of what we learned or discussed? (Think especially about the examples you listed during the final activity.)

Then close with the following prayer or one of your choosing:

Lord, thank you for the time we've had together today to learn from Scripture, from Dr. Seuss, and from one another. Give us the strength and patience not to give in to envy and resentment, but to look for all the ways that your light shines; we pray all these things in Jesus's name. Amen.

Session 2

WHEN CHRISTMAS ISN'T CHRISTMAS

The people of Whoville in *How the Grinch Stole Christmas!* take Christmas very seriously. When the Grinch "steals" their celebration, they discover that Christmas isn't really about decorations, gift-giving, or a lot of the traditional Christmas festivities. Amid the busyness of the Advent and Christmas seasons—especially for students who also have to juggle the end of the school semester—it's easy for us to lose sight of what we're actually celebrating.

During Advent we prepare our hearts for all the ways that Christ enters our world. We prepare to celebrate Christ's birth in Bethlehem more than two thousand years ago. But we also focus on all the ways that

29

Christ continues to enter our world and our lives. Christ is present today through the actions and relationships of his followers.

GETTING READY

For this session you will need:

- Bibles
- A markerboard or large sheet of paper
- Markers
- Pens or pencils

MORE ABOUT…THAN JESUS
(5-10 MINUTES)

Supplies: pens or pencils

As participants arrive, take a few minutes to complete the following sentence with as many examples as possible:

Christmas is often more about _____ **than about Jesus.**

Think of things that, during the Advent and Christmas seasons, often become a higher priority than celebrating Jesus's birth.

After most participants have arrived and have had a couple of minutes to come up with ideas, ask volunteers to read aloud some of their examples.

Then discuss:

- Which of these things are you sometimes guilty of making a greater priority than Jesus during the Advent and Christmas seasons?
- Why do people tend to get worked up about so many things during the Advent and Christmas seasons that have nothing to do with Jesus?

WHEN CHRISTMAS ISN'T CHRISTMAS (5-10 MINUTES)

Supplies: a markerboard or large sheet of paper, markers

Invite a participant to read aloud:

A parody is a "stylized imitation of something generally recognized." If you're familiar with the music of "Weird Al" Yankovic, you've probably heard several song parodies. "Weird Al" and his band replicate popular songs note-for-note but replace the words with comical lyrics.

Together, brainstorm a list of parodies. These can be song parodies, movies that spoof a popular story for comedy or to make a point, or other products that are "stylized imitations" of something else. List these on a markerboard or large sheet of paper. Spend a few minutes on your list then discuss:

- The purpose of most parodies is to make people laugh. Can you think of any parodies that teach a lesson or make a serious point?

Invite a participant to read aloud:

> The Grinch steals Christmas in Whoville by becoming a parody of their Christmas celebrations. He dresses as Santa Claus. He disguises his dog as a reindeer. He finds an old sleigh and a big bag. The Grinch appears as though he'll be playing Santa. Instead, he uses aspects of the Whoville Christmas celebration to steal Christmas. Yet, he fails. Dr. Seuss uses this parody to show that a lot of the decorations and symbols we associate with Christmas don't really matter. Christmas is about much more than trees and tinsel and packages.

LOOKING THE PART (10-15 MINUTES)

Supplies: Bibles, pens or pencils

Divide into teams of three or four. Assign each team one of the following:

- An outdoor Christmas decoration
- An indoor Christmas decoration
- A televised Christmas special
- A popular Christmas song

It is OK if more than one team is assigned the same item. It also is OK if one or more of the items isn't assigned to a team.

Teams should imagine that they have been tasked with designing a decoration, producing a television special, or writing a song. Their objectives are to create something that most people will immediately associate with Christmas and that will be popular. (Teams designing a decoration should come up with something they would imagine a lot of people buying; teams coming up with a song or a TV special should come up with something they would imagine a lot of people listening to or watching.) Teams coming up with a popular song don't need to come up with a tune or lyrics but should instead think about the style of song, what instruments would be used, and the subject of the lyrics. Teams coming up with a TV special should describe the plot and possibly name some actors who would be involved.

Allow teams about four minutes to work. Then each team should briefly present its idea to the others. After each presentation, ask:

- What makes this [decoration, special, or song] a Christmas [decoration, special, or song]?
- If people saw or heard this during another time of the year, would they immediately recognize it as a Christmas [decoration, special, or song]?

After all the presentations, discuss:

- Think of all the things that our culture associates with Christmas. What are some things that we associate with Christmas that don't really have anything to do with celebrating Jesus's birth or how God is present with us through Christ?
- Why do you think these things have become associated with Christmas?

Invite a volunteer to read aloud Luke 2:8-16.

Ask another participant to read aloud:

> The first Christmas celebration didn't involve any of the things that the Grinch stole or tried to ruin. There was no Santa Claus, and there were no snowmen nor decorated trees. There were no multicolored lights, and no wrapped presents. There was no planning or build up. Shepherds were having an ordinary night at work when their work was interrupted by the angel's announcement. They found Jesus and his family in a stable they didn't own in a town they didn't live in.

Discuss:

- What can we learn from the first Christmas celebration that we could apply to our Christmas celebrations?

OUTSIDERS (CORRESPONDS WITH "SLEIGH BELLS," 10 MINUTES)

Supplies: Bibles, markerboard or large sheet of paper, markers

Invite a participant to read aloud:

> The Grinch lives alone on Mt. Crumpit and is not a part of the Whoville community. He's an outsider.

As a group, brainstorm a list of stories where an outsider is the hero. Write your list on a markerboard or large sheet of paper. An outsider could be someone who is new to a school or community, someone who doesn't fit in because of cultural differences, or someone who beats the odds to succeed when most expect them to fail.

Take a few minutes to brainstorm then discuss:

- Why do you think there are so many popular stories about outsiders?

Ask a participant to read aloud:

> The Christmas story is all about outsiders. Mary and Joseph come from Nazareth, a small town that is a long way from the Temple in Jerusalem or the seat of government in Rome. The first people to hear the good news of Jesus's birth were shepherds, ordinary workers without access to power or wealth. Matthew's Gospel tells us of another group of outsiders who traveled a long way to celebrate the birth of the Christ Child.

Discuss:

- We refer to Jesus as our "Messiah." What does it mean for Jesus to be our Messiah?

Invite a participant to read aloud:

> The word *messiah* literally means "anointed one" or "God's anointed." Jesus was Jewish and lived among a Jewish community. Many (but not all) Jews looked forward to the day when God would send a messiah to restore the kingdom of Israel. There were different beliefs about what this messiah would look like and do, but the idea of a messiah comes from Judaism.

A participant should reread aloud Matthew 2:1-12. (You read these verses during the previous session.)

Discuss:

- What does Matthew tell us about those who visited young Jesus in Bethlehem?

Invite a participant to read aloud:

Matthew describes these visitors as "magi" who "came from the east." He doesn't tell us much more than that. He doesn't even tell us how many there are. But based on this description, along with the fact that they are following a star, we can guess that they come from Persia and are skilled in astrology. And we can be pretty certain that they are not Jewish and do not come from territory controlled by Herod or the Roman Empire. They likely aren't familiar with stories of Moses, the words of the Old Testament prophets, or the struggles of God's people. Yet they are drawn to Jesus, the newborn Messiah. This suggests that Jesus is a messiah not only for the Jewish people, but for all people.

HE CHOSE...WISELY (10 MINUTES)

Supplies: Bibles

The title of this section comes, not from *How the Grinch Stole Christmas!*, but from the movie *Indiana Jones and the Last Crusade*. If any participants are familiar with the scene in which Indiana Jones must select which of many cups is the Holy Grail, have them summarize it for the group.

Ask a participant to read aloud:

> Indiana Jones successfully chooses the Grail because, unlike the villains in the story, he isn't taking it for himself. He wants to save his father and keep the Grail out of the hands of the Nazis. During the Advent season we often celebrate another person whose work was focused on something greater than himself.

Invite a volunteer to read aloud Matthew 3:1-12.
Discuss:

- What do these verses tell us about John the Baptist?
- According to verse 3, what role does John play in Jesus's ministry?

A participant should read aloud:

> In the 2000 film version of *How the Grinch Stole Christmas*, Cindy Lou Who is the only resident of Whoville who seems to realize that the Whos have lost the true meaning of Christmas and have made the holiday all about themselves. She points to a better way of celebrating and advocates for including the Grinch. Cindy Lou plays a John the Baptist role. She holds the people of Whoville accountable and prepares them for something greater.

In the spirit of Cindy Lou Who and John the Baptist (and Indiana Jones), think of an activity that you really love doing. What does it look like when you do this activity for your own glory? What does it look like when you do this activity for God's glory and/or for the good of others? Reflect on these questions for a few minutes. Then each person should:

- Describe what it looks like to do something that they love selfishly and for their own glory. (For example, if the activity is basketball, this could involve focusing on individual stats instead of on the success of the team.)

- Describe what it looks like to do something that they love for the glory of God and/or the good of others. (For example, if the activity is playing video games, it could involve making time to play with a younger child who is having a hard time and needs a way to have fun and get his or her mind off of things.)

Ask a participant to read aloud:

> As followers of Christ, our actions should point to Christ. We do this by showing our love of God and of others in all that we do.

WHEN THERE IS NO HOPE
(20 MINUTES)

Supplies: Bibles, pens and pencils

Dr. Seuss used poetry to tell many of his stories. His use of rhyme and meter has given us many famous and memorable lines. See how many of the following Dr. Seuss quotes you can complete by filling in the blank.

1. "A person's a _____, no matter how small."
   —*Horton Hears a Who*

2. "One fish, two fish, _____ fish, _____ fish."
   —[title same as quote]

3. "My trouble was I had a _____ but I couldn't make it up."
   —*Hunches in Bunches*

4. "Maybe Christmas, the Grinch thought, doesn't come from a

   _____."

   —*How the Grinch Stole Christmas!*

5. "You're off to Great Places! Today is your day!

   Your _____ is waiting, So… get on your way!"

   —*Oh, the Places You'll Go!*

The answers for this activity are on page 61.

Ask a participant to read aloud:

The Old Testament prophets also used poetry to get their points across.

Ask another volunteer to read aloud Isaiah 11:6-9. In these verses the prophet Isaiah gives us a glimpse of the peace of God's kingdom.

In these verses Isaiah names several pairs of creatures that, under normal circumstances, would not do well together. Take a couple of minutes to list, in the space below, some other additional unlikely pairs. These pairs are not limited to animals but may also include humans whom we would not expect to coexist peacefully.

After a couple of minutes, invite volunteers to name some of the examples they listed.

Then ask a participant to read aloud:

> During the Advent season we not only prepare to celebrate Jesus's birth, but we also prepare our hearts for all the ways that Christ enters our world and makes God's kingdom a reality. The prophet Isaiah, John the Baptist, and even Cindy Lou Who show us that we experience God's kingdom through peace, reconciliation, and living in right relationship with one another.

CLOSING (5-10 MINUTES)

Discuss:

- What is one thing you learned during our time together that you didn't know before?
- What is one thing that you will do in the coming week as a result of what we learned or discussed? (Think especially about the examples you listed during the final activity.)

Then close with the following prayer or one of your choosing:

Lord, thank you for the time we've had together today to learn from Scripture, from Dr. Seuss, and from one another. During this Advent season focus our hearts on Christ and on experiencing God's kingdom here and now; we pray all these things in Jesus's name. Amen.

Session 3

WHEN LIGHT SHINES

When the Grinch decides to steal Christmas from Whoville, he dresses as Santa Claus. Santa Claus is famous for being jolly and generous. He makes and delivers gifts to children throughout the world on Christmas morning. But there's a catch! Santa Claus keeps track of children's behavior. He knows who has been good and who has been bad. Good children get the gifts they desire. Bad children get coal or sticks or nothing at all. Santa holds children accountable for their behavior.

God also holds us accountable for our behavior. Unlike Santa Claus, God doesn't withhold gifts. Instead, God offers us grace. Through Christ, God redeems and transforms us. The redemption we have through Christ is similar to the redemption of the Grinch at the end of *How the Grinch Stole Christmas!* When the people of Whoville continue their Christmas celebration without all of the gifts and decorations that the Grinch had taken, the Grinch turns away from his anger and jealousy. He feels his heart grow, and he joins the Whos in their holiday festivities.

GETTING READY

For this session you will need:

- Bibles
- A markerboard or large sheet of paper
- Markers
- Pens or pencils

YOU BETTER WATCH OUT (5 MINUTES)

As participants arrive, discuss how Santa Claus affected your behavior when you were younger. (You might also include the Elf on the Shelf in this discussion.) Did you ever decide not to do something because you didn't want to get in trouble with Santa? Did you ever worry that something you did (or didn't do) would affect what gifts you received on Christmas morning?

Then discuss:

- What people, or what factors, have the biggest effect on your behavior? How so?

WHEN LIGHT SHINES (5-10 MINUTES)

Supplies: Bibles

Discuss:

42

- How much light do you need to get to sleep? (For instance, do you prefer complete darkness? Do you have a night light? Do you prefer for the television to be on?)
- What is the value, or purpose, of having a night light?
- Fear of the dark is a common phobia. What is so frightening about the dark?

Invite a participant to read aloud:

> The Grinch steals Whoville's Christmas gifts and decorations in the dark of night, when he is least likely to be seen.

Invite one or two volunteers to read aloud Acts 26:12-18.

In these verses the apostle Paul is telling the story of his first encounter with Christ.

Discuss:

- What role do light and darkness play in Paul's story?

TELLING THE TRUTH (10 MINUTES)

Supplies: Bibles

Discuss:

- Is anyone familiar with Belsnickel, a figure from Christmas traditions in German-speaking cultures?

Ask a participant to read aloud:

> According to German legend, Belsnickel would dress in fur and deliver Christmas gifts to children. A couple of weeks before

43

Christmas, he would check to make sure that the children were behaving. He would knock on a window or door with a stick. He would ask children to answer a question or sing a song then would reward them by throwing candy onto the floor. If children lunged too quickly for the candy, Belsnickel would strike them with his stick.

Discuss:

- Why, do you think, are so many cultures drawn to figures like Santa Claus or Belsnickel who hold children accountable for their behavior?

- Who are the people in your life who hold you accountable for your behavior—not only at Christmastime but throughout the year?

Ask a participant to read aloud:

In *How the Grinch Stole Christmas!*, the Grinch dresses as Santa Claus to take Christmas away from the Whos. He isn't interested in holding the Whos accountable for their behavior. He wants to make them pay for how they make him feel. On Christmas morning, when the Whos continue their celebration without decorations or gifts, they teach the Grinch a lesson and hold him accountable for his envy and resentment.

Ask a volunteer to read aloud Acts 9:10-20. "Saul" in these verses is the apostle Paul. When we first meet Paul in the Book of Acts, he is referred to as "Saul."

Discuss:

- What does God ask Ananias to do?

44

- How does Ananias respond?
- What is the result of Ananias's work?

Invite a volunteer to read aloud:

> Paul had been notorious for persecuting Christians. He had been bad. But he wasn't punished with coal or sticks in his Christmas stocking. God had other plans for Paul and worked through Ananias to hold Paul accountable and nudge him in a new direction. God doesn't excuse bad, sinful behavior. But God offers us grace and redemption and provides people such as Ananias who can guide and correct us. God also calls us to play this role in the lives of others.

EVEN THE CRUMBS WERE TOO SMALL
(10 MINUTES)

Supplies: Bibles, pens or pencils

In the space below, spend two minutes listing any items you own that you don't really need or use but that you refuse to throw out or give away. This could include clothing, old toys, things that no longer work, old awards, and so forth.

After two minutes, allow volunteers to read some of the items on their lists. Then discuss:

- Why do you think people get so attached to things? Why do people have trouble giving away or throwing away what they don't need?

Ask a volunteer to read aloud:

When the Grinch "stole" Christmas from Whoville, he took everything Christmas-related from every house, leaving only crumbs behind. All of the food, lights, ornaments, and wrapped gifts that they had so carefully set out disappeared over night. The Grinch took all the "trimmings" and all the "trappings." But on Christmas morning, the Whos of Whoville woke up and sang joyfully. The decorations and presents didn't really matter to them in the end, as much as the joy they found in celebrating Christmas together.

Invite a volunteer to read aloud Matthew 6:19-21, which comes from Jesus's Sermon on the Mount.

Discuss:

- What does Jesus mean by "treasures...on earth"?
- Why is it pointless for us to store up "earthly" treasures?
- What are some examples of "treasures...in heaven" (verse 20)?
- What does the story of the Grinch and the people of Whoville teach about earthly and heavenly treasures?

46

WHEN YOU'RE SURE YOU'RE RIGHT
(10 MINUTES)

Supplies: Bibles, pens or pencils

Invite a participant to read aloud:

> Dr. Seuss doesn't explain why the Grinch hates the Whoville Christmas celebration so much. The Grinch just seems to resent the Whos and how much they enjoy the holiday.

Invite a volunteer to read aloud Matthew 2:1-4, 12, and 16.

Ask another participant to read aloud:

> Herod had very little information about the "newborn king of the Jews" whom the magi spoke of. But he still felt threatened by the news. Like the Grinch he was resentful, and he decided to act out.

Discuss:

- How did Herod respond after the magi refused to lead him to the "newborn king of the Jews"?
- What might have been a more rational way for Herod to have responded?

In the space at the top of the following page, describe a time when you became angry and resentful because of someone else's joy or success. (You don't need to name anyone's name or provide specific details.)

Briefly describe how you responded to this situation. Thinking back, how could you have handled the situation differently, or better?

Volunteers may describe the situation they chose, how they responded, and what they could have done differently. But no one should feel pressured to share.

Invite a participant to read aloud:

> If we let envy and resentment get the best of us, we tend to act in ways that are destructive and that damage our relationship with God and with others. When we feel these emotions, we

need to draw on the Holy Spirit and look to those people who hold us accountable so that we can deal with our feelings instead of acting out.

THE MANGER OF LOVE (5 MINUTES)

Supplies: Bibles

After Mary learned that she would be the mother of God's Son, the Messiah, and after Mary had shared the news with her relative Elizabeth, she sang a song of praise.

Invite one or two volunteers to read aloud Luke 1:46-55.

We traditionally refer to the song in these verses as the "Magnificat." Magnificat is Latin for the word in verse 46 that appears as "magnifies" or "glorifies" in English translations.

Discuss:

• How does Mary describe God in the "Magnificat"?
• According to Mary, what sorts of things is God doing?

Ask a participant to read aloud:

Mary sings about God lifting up people of low status, such as those who are hungry and those without power. Throughout Scripture God works through people whom we might consider ordinary or unexpected to do the work of God's kingdom. In the 2000 movie version of *How the Grinch Stole Christmas*, the hero is a child, Cindy Lou Who. She is the one who makes peace between the Grinch and the people of Whoville. A person doesn't have to be famous, powerful, or wealthy to have a big impact on his or her community and world.

CLOSING (5-10 MINUTES)

Discuss:

- What is one thing you learned during our time together that you didn't know before?
- What is one thing that you will do in the coming week as a result of what we learned or discussed? (Think especially about the examples you listed during the final activity.)

Then close with the following prayer or one of your choosing:

Lord, thank you for the time we've had together today to learn from Scripture, from Dr. Seuss, and from one another. Thank you for the people in our lives who guide us and hold us accountable. As we approach Christmas, give us the strength to let go of earthly treasures and store up treasures in heaven; we pray all these things in Jesus's name. Amen.

Session 4

WHEN JOY IS OUR SONG

One of the words most commonly associated with Christmas is *joy*. We sing, "Joy to the World," because the long-awaited Messiah has come. We remember the joy that Mary felt as the mother of the newborn Christ Child. And we look forward to the joy of spending time with family, opening gifts, and getting some time away from school.

Of course, joy is not the only feeling we experience in the days and weeks leading up to Christmas. Joy is sometimes mixed with anxiety, frustration, and even sadness. Mary and Joseph had the stress of an unplanned pregnancy and a long journey. In *How the Grinch Stole Christmas!*, all of the Whos' gifts and decorations are stolen by a grumpy guy dressed up like Santa Claus. But, in both cases, joy prevails. For the Grinch, joy leads to his redemption, and he joins the celebration.

Getting Ready

For this session you will need:

- Bibles
- A markerboard or large sheet of paper
- Markers
- Pens or pencils

Gifts That Can't Be Wrapped
(5 MINUTES)

As participants arrive, discuss some Christmas gifts you'd like to receive that cannot be wrapped and opened on Christmas morning. Try to be as specific as possible. For example, don't say "world peace" or "an end to hunger." Instead, you might hope for the end of a certain specific conflict, or wish that a local ministry will get the resources it needs to provide Christmas meals for those who don't have them. (Your Christmas wishes do not need to be as noble as peace or ending hunger. You might also ask for the gifts of getting an "A" in geometry or seeing a favorite sports team qualify for the postseason.)

When most people are present and have had a chance to contribute, discuss:

- How do these potential gifts compare to other things that you'd like to receive for Christmas? Which would you be more excited about getting?
- What can you do to make some of these unwrapped gifts a reality? (For instance, if you wished for an end to homelessness,

how could you get involved with efforts to provide homes and shelter for those who need it?)

HOW CAN I KEEP FROM SINGING?
(10 MINUTES)

Supplies: Bibles, pens or pencils

Write, in the space below, the name of a song that you like to listen to when you are...

- ...celebrating.

- ...upset.

- ...trying to hype yourself up.

- ...trying to relax.

Discuss:

- What other songs do you like to listen to in certain situations because they create a certain mood?
- Why do you think music has such an effect on our moods?

Ask a participant to read aloud:

In *How the Grinch Stole Christmas!* the Grinch hears singing coming from Whoville on Christmas morning. He'd expected the Whos to be angry or in mourning, but they are singing. In the original story Dr. Seuss doesn't say what song they were singing or what it was about, but the song is an expression of joy and love. Their singing signifies that Christmas is not about gifts and decorations but about peace and hope and relationships.

Scripture includes several examples of God's people performing songs of praise and celebration. In the previous session, we read the "Magnificat," which Mary sings after learning that she will be the mother of the Christ Child.

Ask a volunteer to read aloud Exodus 15:20-21.

Invite a participant to read aloud:

Miriam was Moses's sister and one of the leaders of the Israelites. After God delivered Israel from slavery in Egypt and parted the sea so that they could escape on dry land, Moses led the Israelites in a song of praise. Miriam played the tambourine and led the women of Israel in song as well. Throughout history, music has been an important part of how God's people worship and express praise and thanksgiving.

THE HEART THAT GREW THREE SIZES (10 MINUTES)

Supplies: pens or pencils

Think of a moment when everything changed for you, and write about it in the space below. This could involve a big opportunity that changed your life in a big way, but it also could be an experience that caused you to think or feel differently.

After a couple of minutes, volunteers may read aloud what they wrote. Then invite a participant to read aloud:

> Dr. Seuss had described the Grinch as having a heart that was "two sizes too small." When the Grinch heard the Whos celebrating, even without their gifts and decorations, something changed. His heart grew three sizes. John Wesley, an eighteenth-century pastor and theologian and the founder of Methodism, famously had an experience similar to what happens to the Grinch on Christmas morning. In 1738, while Wesley was attending a prayer meeting and listening to a reading of Martin Luther's commentary on Romans, he felt his heart "strangely warmed." In that moment, he felt an assurance that he could fully trust in Christ for his salvation and that, by God's grace, he was free from sin and death. While not everyone experiences a moment of radical transformation like the Grinch or John Wesley, we all have the assurance that God's grace is at work in our lives, changing and perfecting us.

THE HEART THAT GREW THREE SIZES: YOUTH STUDY BOOK

PEACE WITH JUSTICE *(10 MINUTES)*

Supplies: Bibles, a markerboard or large sheet of paper, markers

Write these two sentence starters, each in a separate column, on a markerboard or large sheet of paper.

Forgiveness is...   Forgiveness is not...

As a group, brainstorm ways to complete the sentences, thinking of what you do or don't do when you forgive someone.

Then invite a participant to read aloud:

> If we truly forgive someone, we no longer hold grudges or seek revenge. This does not mean that we excuse that person's behavior or that what they did becomes OK. The Grinch was wrong to have "stolen" Christmas from the Whos. Despite this bad behavior, the Whos invite the Grinch to join their Christmas celebration. On the final page of *How the Grinch Stole Christmas!* the Grinch is carving the roast beast at the Whos' Christmas dinner.

Ask a volunteer to read aloud Matthew 5:43-48.
Discuss:

- In these verses Jesus instructs us to love our enemies. How does Jesus make the case that we should love people who hate or harass us?

AT THE TABLE *(10 MINUTES)*

Supplies: Bibles

Invite a participant to read aloud:

56

How the Grinch Stole Christmas! ends with the Grinch carving the roast beast at Christmas dinner. The picture in the book shows a Christmas wreath behind the Grinch's head, situated so that it looks like a halo. We don't know if Dr. Seuss did this intentionally, but it's a nice image. On that last page, we see that the villain of the story has been redeemed and is seated at the head of the table.

Divide the group into two teams. Each team will read a teaching of Jesus involving a banquet, then answer the following questions:

- What lesson is Jesus teaching?
- Why do you think Jesus uses the example of a banquet to teach this lesson?
- How can we apply Jesus's teaching to our lives today?

The two Scriptures are:

- Team 1: Luke 14:7-14
- Team 2: Luke 14:15-24

Give each team about four minutes to read and discuss. Then invite each team to summarize its Scripture and its answers to the questions.

THE ANGEL OF JOY (10-15 MINUTES)

Supplies: Bibles, pens or pencils

Ask a participant to read aloud:

In the end of *How the Grinch Stole Christmas!* Whoville is at peace. The Grinch fails to steal Christmas, experiences redemption, and joins the celebration. But earlier in the story, peace seems unlikely. The Grinch hopes to cause pain and sadness and appears to be on his way toward doing exactly that. The Christmas story has a similar feel. Each year we sing, "Sleep in heavenly peace." But the events leading up to Jesus's birth do not seem headed toward a peaceful resolution.

Read each of the following Scriptures about the chaotic events leading up to Jesus's birth. For each one, make a note below of any words of assurance, words that offer peace amid chaos.

Scriptures: **Words of Assurance:**

Matthew 1:18-25

Luke 1:5-17

Luke 2:26-38

Luke 2:39-45

Ask volunteers to read aloud the examples of "words of assurance" they recorded. Then discuss:

- How do you think Mary and Joseph and the other figures in these Scriptures responded to these words of assurance? What might they have been thinking when they were told not to fear or that they were blessed?

58

- When has someone said something to you that brought you peace during a chaotic time?
- When have you been in a situation to bring peace or assurance to a stressful situation?

Ask a participant to read aloud:

> God doesn't promise us an easy, carefree life. But God offers us peace and assurance in troubled times. God also works through us to offer peace and assurance to others.

CLOSING (5-10 MINUTES)

Discuss:

- What is one thing you learned during our time together that you didn't know before?
- What is one thing that you will do in the coming week as a result of what we learned or discussed? (Think especially about the examples you listed during the final activity.)

Then close with the following prayer or one of your choosing:

Lord, thank you for the time we've had together today to learn from Scripture, from Dr. Seuss, and from one another. Open our eyes, ears, and minds to the joy that we have through Christ, even amid the stress and busyness of the season. We pray all these things in Jesus's name. Amen.

ANSWERS

To "Pop Quiz" on pages 16–17:

1. Theodor Geisel
2. 1957
3. Dr. Seuss himself
4. 1966, on CBS
5. Jim Carrey
6. Just *The Grinch*
7. Benedict Cumberbatch

To "When There Is No Hope" on pages 38–39:

1. person
2. red, blue
3. mind
4. store
5. mountain

CPSIA information can be obtained
at www.ICGtesting.com
Printed in the USA
LVHW040102291021
701807LV00005B/9

9 781791 017415